KKGentertainment & Enterprises Presents: Kontagious Memoirs, Spoken Word, and Poetry,

Life Span at a glance

By: Professor Coker Jerome George (a.k.a. KKG)

"Life Span Development is who and what we are"
(Kontagious Quote)

KKGentertainment & Enterprises, Memphis, TN
(KKG Publishing & Editing, CEO, (Eldad) Coker Jerome George)

Visit: Coker George website:

1) Kontagiousgift.blogspot.com
2) thechangeiam.blogspot.com
3) thecookshop.blogspot.com
4) kkgathleticshwf.blogspot.com
5) KKGentertainmentandenterprises.blogspot.org

Visit: http://kkgentertainment.wix.com/kkg-entertainment-page

To purchase the book, visit Barnes and Nobles.com and Amazon.com

For Life span at a glance apparel visit: http://www.zazzle.com/life_span_at_glance_tee _shirt_design_1-235320027983094473

Youtube: Verses of the Soul,

Facebook: Coker Jerome George – group - Verses of the Soul

-Kontagious Writings

Twitter: Kontagiousdem

Instagram:Kontagiousgift

All material in this book is registered trademarks of KKGentertainment & Enterprises

All material in the book Copyright 2013 by: Coker Gerome George

Designed by: Coker Jerome George a.k.a. KKG, KKG Publishing & Editing

Published in 2014 as Life Span at a Glance

Dedication

Nothing is too hard for God. To my children, Elijah, Elizabeth, Elizabeth, and Eli, I say daddy love you. It is because of my parents, my mother and father, and God first, that I am the man I am today. To my wife Erica, thanks for being a true exemplary of what a wife and mother should be, mine Proverbs 31 woman. We are village and we cannot do anything alone, without the help of God and family.

Chapter 1

Becoming a man

The age of twenty one was a fascinating age for me, for many reasons I must say. My junior year in college was great, in that if I could do it all over again, I would take away the stresses that came with that age however. I experienced so much growth and development in the twenty first years of my life. I had just recently pledge my fraternity, Kappa Alpha Psi incorporated and Greek life was amazing. I have always been well known, in that I am a very extroverted individual. I was achieving in every field of human endeavor and was on my way of matriculating out of college. Socially and culturally I was active on campus and in the East Austin community as far as politics and service goes. The attention and exposure I experienced at this age was life changing and those experiences groomed me for who I am now.

Twenty one is the best age to be because you are at the introductory prime of your life and the world is in the palm of your hands and you can shape your life however you choose. I have seen many people finish college at this age or drop out of college at this age. Socially you are just able to start drinking legally at this stage of your life and you can wild out as much as you choose but it is up you to be wise.

Life did change for me at age twenty one though, my fraternity chapter got in trouble at my school and that forced us to grow up real fast. According to Santrock (2007) "Nonnegative life events are unusual occurrences that have a major impact on the individual's life. Examples include the death of a parent when a child is young, pregnancy in early adolescence a fire that destroys a home, winning the lottery, or getting an unexpected career opportunity with special privileges." We were investigated and great deal of distress came with that. During this depressing period, I lost six relatives, extended but close enough in one month. I lost an uncle to kidney failure and an extended uncle and four cousins in an apartment fire. My world was at pause but it forced me to grow up. I would not change these experiences because that is how God intended life to be, in calling them home and teaching me in a way to mature.

Chapter 2

I use to work at the boy's and girl's club in Trenton, New Jersey, one of the most
challenging cities economically, socially, and developmentally a child can come
up in. The disparity here is through the roof, much like other settings similar to
Trenton around the country. As some may or may not know, Trenton is one of the
developmentally deprived cities in the nations, as far as everything, especially
when it comes to the education system. The social disorganization that exists in
the city is enormous. Young people are not held to high expectation in the school
districts or systems. As an associate director of the teen program, one often came
across young people in these school systems, which graduating from high school
became a grand milestone for. Many of these young people reading levels are four
or even five grades lower than their actual grades. It's a sad situation but this is
the great nation we live in, where similar instances are exemplified throughout the
country.

The legal age of eighteen as agreed upon by law is a questionable age to say. At
eighteen one is able to cognitively decide what the best choices are to make at this
stage in life. According to Santrock (2007) "cognitive processes involve changes
in the individual's thought, intelligence, and language." As a young adult you
should have now gotten the concepts your parents have been trying to instill in you
from your early childhood. This is the time the application of those good home
training and skills mom and dad as well your family members have been striving

to embed in you. As a young person at the age of eighteen, you are looking forward to college and all the fun and growth that comes along with that age but however a great deal of responsibility must be accompany as well.

Chapter 3

What happened at age 22-27

I was engaged at 22, really young, and I had a partner who had not experienced much in life, specifically not being on her own or really detached from home. I myself was not experienced when it came to a serious relationship and stepping into a marriage. We started making wedding plans and she pretty much took over the plans and we ended up falling out, lifestyles not being compatible and things not working out. I was saved by divine intervention from jumping into the situation of marriage at an early age. That toxicity that was building would have eventually led to divorce, an awful way to start life off I believe. According to Baldwin and Wray (2007)"The first principle of a life-span perspective on social status and health is that social status can affect health at any point from birth (or even before) until death" (Settersten, 2003). I was deeply in love with this young lady, having dated since our freshmen year in a college, a long distance relationship, that had finally come together, us being in the same setting after four years of being distant. She being a member of Alpha Kappa Alpha Sorority Incorporated and me being a Nupe, a member of Kappa Alpha Psi Fraternity Incorporated, seemed like a match made in Heaven, on paper. In reality we were too different people, whose goals, aspirations, and vision for life didn't quite align.

I have always had that fierce adaucity of hope to make it on a big time scale, wanting to get the most out of life, in that I was groomed to believe, what you put in life is what you will get out. An opportunity came along and I met Kat Williams and we became friends and ask me to become his confidant and assistant. I sought the opportunity, somewhat of bad timing on my part, leaving the week of Thanksgiving, writing her a note because my phone had just broken but then having to come back to house and seeing her, with all hell breaking loose. We fell out, I left with she giving me an altimatum, returning a week later because of guilt, for things to fall completely out. We would be seperated for a few months, trying to hash things out, and then to find out from a fraternity brother of mine that xyz had happened in my absence. Emotionally and physically I blocked the experience out my mind and moved on to the next phase of my life, staying in Columbia for a short period and then making that move to Charlotte, North Carolina, where some healing took place. I would go on to date, having series of short term relationships, most of them, if not all them failing due to lack of trust and not letting myself heal properly from the broken heart I experienced in my first failed in engagement, to just being lost emotionally and seeking to fill that void with the next up next relationship mindset. The saying goes, hurt people hurt people, and I can honestly admit that I did my share of heart breaking in seeking true love. In and out, or around love I would go, to then getting engaged a second time; this time financially unstable while in love, while finishing graduate school, I would get my heart terminally broken, spirit, and heart, with the cycle of emotional distraught continuing, until I met my wife Erica George, the spring 2013. This would be the relationship that saved my life, help heal me, renovating my confidence, and my focus on my career.

The belief now in our society is that the age of thirty is an appropriate age to begin life. For most individuals their professional lives are just kicking off and they are starting to grab life concepts from an understanding and collective perspective. At the age of thirty I hope to be completely settled by the grace of God and have some children a well. But as I stated in my previous argument, twenty one is the best age, it is an introductory age to freedom and confusion. Life decisions and which way you can turn, plans about furthering your education and whether to start a family at an early age and all of that comes into play. Thirty is a turning point in life in which an individual look at his or her life and decide this is where I believe I should be headed.

Chapter 4

Falling in love with Psychology

The subject of psychology has really drawn my attention in my education endeavor. I fell in love with psychology at the end of my freshmen year, while interning with the University of Tenn psychology department, during the HCOP program. Cognitive theory which deals with an individual intellectual ability along with language is a theory I believe best explains development. As humanity we are thinking beings that are constantly developing. We learn through experiences and it due to our individual ability to comprehend life circumstance and ability to adapt to these changes that make a person self-actualize into the person he or she can become.

According Santrock (2007, ch 1) *Cognitive processes* involve changes in the individual's thought, intelligence, and language. An individual environment plays a major role in his or development. A child who is exposed to a highly intellectual atmosphere will be more likely to absorb the positivity from that environment, unlike a child who is brought up in an unfortunate none-intellectual atmosphere.

Take for instance a minority child who is brought up in a poverty environment much like most inner city children, compared to a privileged child raised in a suburban neighborhood with all the educational opportunities provided. The suburban raised child thought process will be ahead of that of his or her inner city counterpart. Santrock (2007, ch1) states, that Jean Piaget stressed the fact that humans use cognition to adapt to their environments. Thus, the cognitive theoretical perspective best explains the nature of human development because we are evolving beings.

We do in fact evolve due to our environment and adapt to our surroundings based on what is occurring. Our interaction with our peers in our early development does play a major role in who become. Example being, making fun of others who are less fortunate is an excellent point. As youths we do try to fit in with our peers, based on what they are doing. We think about what we must do to be accepted by our peers and thus in turn, perceive to move forward making the necessary steps that will make us fit into that peer group we want to become apart off.

Children learn a great deal from their environments. As parents, you become chosen educators for your children by humanity. The lessons and exposure you open your child or children up too, is totally up to you. Whether these exposures are positive or negative have an effect on that child cognitive development. As children become older and start going to school and becoming involved in activities and spend more time with their peer groups, their level of exposure broadens. The positive life lessons you try to instill in them from the onset of their lives, whether they choose positive or negative becomes the time period for them to display the rearing and training as well as self-control they have been taught from home.

The field of psychology is wonderful in that the expansion of theories and creations of new theories, based on other theoretical research is what makes the study and discovery of psychology great. I have been fascinated with the cognitive theory since my early study of psychology beginning from my freshmen year in college. The human brain and how we think and function on a high level for the most part is intriguing. Due to my Christian belief, leaning towards the cognitive theory makes great sense, in that we are made in the image and likeness of God, being highly intellectual beings.

Children in fact do learn by experiences. When a child is young and you chastise he or she for doing something wrong, they acknowledges that chastisement and will not repeat that act again, most often. When a negative act goes unpunished in a child's development, they perceive that as an act that is permissible by mom and dad. Cognitive theory does state that as humans we learn by experiences because we are thinking beings. We can all recall, the first time, if ever, when you burned your hand on the stove and how it felt. It became an experience that you did not want to encounter anymore as a being. You learn that when the stove is hot it hurts when you touch it, in that the act should not be repeated again. Thus, stating this point, the theory of cognition makes sense and is argue-ably one of the best theories in describing and studying human development.

Chapter 5
Protect the Sponge

We come into this world as sponges that have not yet been soaked into water. Once exposed to the environment that we are brought up in, we then become like sponges that have been soaked into a sink full of water. Children are thinking beings that are constantly evolving each and every day as they grow. The role of environment in a child's life is instrumental, in that it along with the upbringing instilled in that child by parents modes that particular child or person for life.

Jean Paiget theory of development in comparison to that of Vygotsky's, have four stages of development. According to Santrock (2007), Paiget believed that children construct their understanding of the world and go through four stages of development. Providing your child with a positive environment during his or her upbringing is monumental to that child cognitive development. In working at the Boy's and Girl's Club of America I was able to see the positive effects such programs have on the lives of young children and people. Compared to children their age who are not exposed to the different activities, children in our program were provided the opportunity to achieve and excel. Vygotsky's theory according to Santrock (2007), explains that sociocultural cognitive theory emphasizes how culture and social interaction guide cognitive development. Children social interaction do play a major in their development but it is through those four stages of development as Paiget states that children evolve, through the interaction and influences of their environments.

Both Paiget and Vygotsy theories are excellent in stating the role cognition and environments have in the lives of children. It is just that Paiget breakdown of the transitions of one stage to another makes a lot of sense. In working at the Boy's and Girl's Club with the 4th through 8th graders I was able to see the break down explanation of Paiget theories. According to Santrock (2007), the concrete operational stage is when these children are able to reason logically about events that are occurring in their lives. I saw this on a day to day basis, in that when children know what you expect of them, they may still test you to see if you will constantly hold them to these expectations daily.

Children who are exposed and provided a head start in early education often are able to perform better when they start school. Some children are however innately gifted intellectually though. I can give a few great examples, that of some of my relatives. Not placed into early child education programs by their parents, due to naive parenting skills, the children exemplified that they were naturally intellectual and are able to achieve on a high academic level as they started school. In most instances, statically this is not the case. Had they had been exposed to head start education; I believe they could have been labeled as geniuses. The interaction they had at home with their older cousins, aunts, and uncles, as well as coming from a intellectual blood line enabled them to be as smart as they are, one can assume.

The holding of children hands through life, is an act that just cripples that child or individual for life. As Piaget stated, children evolve due to their environments. As a parent you can prepare your children for experiences life presents them, by telling him or her of some of the similar experiences you have dealt with. Life in itself is unpredictable and no two experiences are ever alike. No matter how much preparation you have gone through, each individual will react differently to each situation as life presents them to him or her.

Children are in fact influenced by their peers especially when they start school. As parents, the time you spend with you children at home, before they start school and while they are in school is meaningful. Our children spend more time with their peers than they do with us, once they start school. The time spent with their peers is influential in their development and how and who they become in life. You child or children learn positive and negative behaviors from their peers. So, if you have failed as a parent to instill positive attributes in your child, they may just stray from you when they start interacting with their peers.

You have to deal with each child differently because they are individuals. Some children are hyperactive and smarter than other children, and others are calm and not as smart as their peers. There is a great range of variation when it comes to children as well as people. Patience is a virtue that we all must learn to attain when dealing with our fellow mankind, particularly children. Some people are gifted to be patient people and others must learn and develop that skill over a period of time.

I often tell people and say that a setback is a setup for a comeback. Young Children brains are like a sponge and they absorb any and everything, especially in their earliest stages of development. Some children are fortunate enough to have been exposed to an intellectual atmosphere at a real young age, for instance a parent in school who allows the child to accompany them during class times, in which this does help to propel that child for life. Once starting school and having been exposed to extensive learning environment, one is often able to become ahead of their peers.

Chapter 6
Neurology in Psychology

The impact that neurological development has had on the past decade has become meaningful too psychology. The most crucial part of human development is the early stages of development. If a child is neurologically affected at birth his or her motor skills may not ever develop or may just develop on a much slower rate that of his or of her peers. Santrock (2007), explains this in the **dynamic systems theory**, that infants assemble motor skills for perceiving and acting. Children perceive the world they are born into, through the interactions they see on a daily basis. If a child nervous system is impaired this is a problem because that child entire psychological outlook of the world is altered.

Thus, the studies of neurology in the most recent decade has been influential in helping aid and bring an end to some of the affects that a lot of children are born with. Stem cell research is instrumental in this field; and poses a big medical breakthrough to a lot of parents who have children born to such unfortunate birth defects. If ever the case presented itself where I was a teacher of education, I would promote my students to research the field of neurology, especially in the areas of stem cell research because I firmly believe that great medical breakthrough can come from this research from the mental aspects as well.

Early childhood is the most important time to correct a neurological disorder. Helping a child before he or she has begun interacting with his or her peers is essential in that child social psychological development as well. These defects are associated a great deal to the life styles a child parents have lived. Before the affect can worsen it can be corrected by means of just paying more and extra attention to that child. Children who are affected by neurological disorder can still develop into normal people with the proper care and nurturing.

From a religious perspective as I previously stated; God uses a situation that seem bad or unfortunate to show and display his glory. Since the turn of the World War II era, it has seem that mankind has lost its religious identity and is quick to give up on individuals that are not brought into the world as the normal child or children. I can remember from my early childhood, I honestly felt that something was wrong with me and that I could not catch on to my school work as quickly as my peers. I was a slow developer in that I lacked focus but as I grew older and my brain neurologically developed, I passed most of mine peers and that eagerness to learn just begin to fire up inside of me.

From birth children need to be loved. It is unfortunate that this does not occur for a great number of children who come into humanity. Due to the lack of love a lot children become deprived emotionally, which leads to psychological problems, from childhood and throughout their adult years. The affect this has on an individual neurological development is instrumental. These same children become adults and this trend is transferred often to their children. It is through the grace of God and divine intervention can such a detrimental trend of psychological poisoning be stopped from my Christian psychology perspective. Children at an early age just need to know that they are loved. Holding a child and speaking positive words into his or her life is meaningful for that child psychological development. Whether you realize it or not, that child absorbs and remember those positive and negative events from their childhood and it will remain embodied and embedded in that child soul, throughout his or her development.

Chapter 7
Emotionality

The development of emotional problems becomes evident in children due to their social upbringings and surroundings, the inclusion being their parents. Children are emotionally affected due to the lives their parents are living and choose to bring them up in. A valid example is that of a child growing up in home, where he or she sees his or her mother and father physically and verbally abusing one another. The emotional trauma associated with such a scenario has a long lasting effect on a child for life.

The transference of emotional trauma to a child is detrimental to that child health and social life as well. What occurs at home does end abroad. This means wherever that child social network extends he or she will be ultimately affected by those experiences endured at home. According to Santrock (2007), Jean Paiget theory of organization explains that in order to make sense of the world children organize their experiences. Every experience a child goes through, especially from their early stages of development affects him or her for life. They in turn grow up to become adults and display these emotional traumatic experiences through their relationships as well as when they themselves have children.

The emotional traumas children do experience do affect their academic performances as stated. It is unfortunate that children often have to get the short end of the stick, when a situation does not have anything to do with that child or children. Parents, who are going through relationship problems with their spouse or significant other, usually take things out on their children, often lashing out on the child. What these parents fail to realize is, that by treating your child or children this way, one is embedded a lifelong lasting effect on that child.

Although emotion is correlated genetically in the brain and based on an individual child temperament; that temperament can be contained and he or she can learn to channel that in a positive way. However, when a child with such an emotional temperament is continuously being enticed by unfortunate situation, such as that of a violent parent or environment, he or she will have problems throughout his or her life, unless they change, due to positive experiences. From birth, as a parent you must instill in your child that he or she will not run over you. That parental fear, as my father like to call it, must be established. That child must understand who is in charge and who holds the authority over whom.   Children are not to dictate to their parents. This problem can be handled at an early age but if it goes unhandled throughout their early stage of development and into their teen years, it's almost a lost cause.

The variable that is playing a role is the parental upbringing of the child. Children play on their parents emotions. A child knows and understands which parent will let him or her get away with what behavior or habit. They often try to play both parties. My mother and father knew this and they stuck firm to each other. When a parent said no to one of us, that was the final answer. We knew we could not go behind daddy back and go ask mom for permission for something, after he had just told us no. They were a team and they kept things under control that way.

Chapter 8
Understanding people

The changes in crystallized and fluid intelligence deals with the understanding of people as individuals, from the psycho-analytic break down of the both level of intelligence. A great example of such case of crystallized intelligence is looking at the lives of the elder family members in your family. For years in the African tradition, the method of crystallized intelligence has been affected.

Traditionally information has been passed down orally for years, from one generation to the next. It is through gaining wisdom and intellect that these elders in the family have been able to perfect such a task. Growing up one of our greatest past times, were just listening to our older relatives talk about stories and events of the past. It was always a joyful moment because we learned of things of the past, that our parents, uncles, and aunts used to engage in. The older relatives never held back the full details of the stories from us, passing the oral history in precise details and imagery. According to Santrock (2007), John Horn believes that some abilities increase in life, while others decrease. My perspective on Horn theory is that it is true. When you are given a gift in life and do not practice it throughout and while you progress in life, you will certainly lose it.

The perspective of fluid intelligence is evident in the lives of individuals who later development serious mental diseases such as Alzheimer's disease. The human brain is a muscle and it must be constantly put to use or it will weaken. Just like any muscle in the body, if it is not worked out regularly, it turns in to flabby muscles, the same occurs in the human brain, if it is not entertained with mental exercise.

Labeling our youth

Moving to the topic of standardized testing, it is now known that some people are generally calm when it comes to taking test, while others let the pressure get to them. A great number of highly intellectual individuals do not always do well on these tests. They however, could out think and smart most individuals who can pass these tests in a stress fill environment. What I firmly believe is that such test do not determines a person intellect or his or her level of education achievement.

The best way to measure an individual intelligence is through a composite test of the subject matter. Students often play the guessing game and strategy on these standardized tests and are able to come on top by scoring their best on these test. I can recall a friend of mine telling me, he drew a pig on his (ACT) test and scored a 26 on the test. Such tactics and methods have been done by many students and have been able to score high on these tests. Standardized testing psychologically affects many students who are intellectually able to achieve academically. These tests are intimidating because so much are measured and are weighed by these tests. Students often tense up and do not perform their best at all. Some people are just not great test takers. Minorities are mostly affected by these tests and many educational scholars have come to believe that these tests are bias. Humans are thinking beings and we are constantly evolving over time. Due to the nature of crystallized intelligence we become highly smart individuals as we grow older. The experiences we go through and encounter in life causes us to become smarter and better thinking beings, if we learn from mistakes of the past and especially used them as references for the future. As we grow older, we do forget a great deal of what we learn but our learning is constantly being multiplied with new experiences the future offers.

Chapter 9

Self-Actualization

We become who we are largely due to the families and cultures that we come from. The Christian belief is that we are created in God's image and he chooses which network of families that we are born into. As far as self, identity, and personality are concerned, we each are uniquely created as God intended for us to be. No two humans are alike when it comes to self, identity, and personality. As persons we may share similar traits but are never the same.

The concept of self, identity, and personality are intertwine and related because they all deal with the individual. An individual characteristic according to Santrock (2007), is what composes a person, that self. Identity is based on who the person choose to become throughout their life which entails what took place through their stages of development. The concept of personality is the overall evolving of an individual over the span of their development. As people our personality consistently changes, due to the environments we are in. The environmental and intellectual cognitive factor is what helps shape a person identity. We are intellectual beings and we become a certain way to fit the environment we live in, an adaptation philosophy of life.

As people we are constantly evolving and we often in life sometimes have set backs, taking us back to the person we used to be. A person cannot truly say, I have been this way my entire life and have not changed a bit. In some circumstances this may be true but as people we are consistently changing.

Children are really smart and we must encourage them constantly. We must make it our duty reminding them that they are smart, holding them to higher expectations, which lets them know that as a parent that you are counting on them to do those things that will make mom and dad proud. Giving positive as well as negative reinforcement when they do good and bad let's a child knows that mom or dad is aware of what i am doing constantly, whether it is good or bad. Having that sense of fear in your child, not the fear of harm but the fear of respect, will help propel your child in the right direction.

The establishment of rules and guidelines with your child is a great method in dealing with the authoritative parenting style. Setting a standard or protocol with your child gives him or her sense of standard to uphold, in dealing with his or her parent. The child with cognitively gather mentally within themselves and say, "This is what mom and dad expects of me and I know if I do this or that, they will be highly disappointed, so I must not do those things."

We develop our identity by circumstances and experiences we endure. We learn by our environmental cultural experiences as some of us are fortunate to be able to. As for me, personally, growing up, the incorporation of African traditions was meaningful. It has become to play a major part in my life, because knowing who you are and where you are truly from, enables you in a direction to where you are headed or want to head in life.

Children begin to develop conceptions of who they want to become in life due the level of exposure they have early in life. A child that is exposed to a highly intellectual and educational environment, will often want to become that intellectual, such as in the case with most children. Take for instance A child that wants to be a doctor. In order for that to take place, that child must be provided those achieving task that will help get him or her through those early education years and into college. He or she may or may not change her mind of becoming a doctor with proper guidance and nurturing. Nurturing go deep and far. A conversation my father and I have often had is about people who don't know where they come from. Due to this outcome, these individuals are really misguided in life because it is really hard to know where you are headed when no knowledge or connection to one's past exists. Having a sense of direction of your past can really lead to your calling for the future and truly your destiny.

Chapter 10
Attachment

The attachment people have from inception with their birth mother's as well as fathers is instrumental to an individual development as a whole. That sense of belonging and knowing that you are cared for dearly is established early in life. According to Santrock (2007), the phases of development begin as such, with the first phase which starts at birth to two months, in which the infant instinctively direct their attachment to human figures. Stage two begins at two too seven months, in which attachment becomes focused on one figure, usually the primary caregiver. Stage three begins at seven too twenty four months, in which specific attachment develop. This begins with increased loco motor skills, the child actively seeking contact with regular caregivers, such as the mother or father. Stage four begins at twenty four months and on, which children become aware of other feelings, goals, and plans and begin to take these into account in forming their own actions.

The factors that affect parent's ability to establish an attachment relationship with an infant in most cases is the lack of time spent with a child. This is the case with a lot of children who come from wealthy backgrounds where parents work long hours and are never home. The same can be said about children of minority backgrounds, instead in the case of these children, they have parents that may work long hours or two jobs and even have fathers who are incarcerated or have neglected their responsibilities as parents completely.

Attachment does however change during the early childhood years in that children evolve and want to become their own people and want to develop bonds and relationships with other peers. As parents one must be flexible I'm child rearing or face rebellion from that individual in various facets, whether it may emotional shut down or physical outburst. Just as one may remember in your upbringing parents sometimes feel indifferent about the peers their children are associating with. Often as parents your parenting approach must adapt to the change of time and you cannot specifically try all the same methods your parents used to raise you as a child because times change and children environment are constantly evolving through the years. The attachment relationship a child has with his or her mother at birth is extremely important. Doctors know this and that's why a child has been historically given to their mother as soon as she gives birth to that child. In the African tradition this is very evident, the mother and child will often take baths together to development that mother and child bonding. It is a beautiful sight to witness. Having a child is a blessing, a gift too many people take for granted. Here in America, the rate that people of the minority culture have kids is high. What is sad is, these kids are not provided with the best opportunities to excel, mostly due to the system, environment, and individuals they have for parents. It is a sad situation when a child is given all the best opportunities life have to offer and then end up falling to the way side of life streets, an exemplary of what we see with Hollywood or famous entertainers child or children. Children innately yearn to have an attachment to their parents, having a healthy psychological life and development and parents and society must provide that. Just as talked about and discussed in the CNN special Black In America 1&2, that sense of belonging and having a close relationship with one's mother and father as well family, enables the individual to be able to provide the same for his or her child or children one day . Individuals who are not able to develop such relationship with their parents and family but in turn are able to provide such care and relationship attachment with their children, are the blessed and fortunate individuals, breaking the stigma and generational curse of fail parenting. The attachment a child has with his or her parent is very important. An example of attachment I will give is that of my little cousin, who is like a niece to me, my first cousin daughter. This child will literally cry her heart out if she is left alone by herself for any period of time. You can pretty much say that she is spoiled. She has gotten so used to having people care for and cuddle her consistently, that she feels weird when it is not displayed always.

Chapter 11
Communication

The issue of bullying has long been a part of society, especially in the education system for years past. Bullying has not only been a problem in school but as well as an issue in the work place. Such issues that have led to bullying are the school shootings that occurred in the late nineties. Shooting such as the Little Rock shootings and the columbine murders became a major issue during those years.

Approaches to stopping these incidences from occurring would be the affective use of peer mediation in the schools as well as workplace. This violence occurs because individuals feel as if they are being taken advantage of. Communication is the key to life and a great break down in American society as well as the world as a whole, is due to the lack of communication. Great wars and violence have occurred throughout centuries due to the lack of display of this crucial concept of life, communication. When things are bothering you in life and you obviously do like the way things are going, the best way to resolve that issue is communication to the other side, letting that individual or group of people know that you do not approve of their behavior. Children who are bullied as youngsters grow up and become authoritative figures or just completely remain in their shells. A great case is that of a cop who joined police department, who was just recently arrested for assaulting a elderly woman while he was intoxicated and off duty. This young man was bullied and made fun of in high school, a complete nerd. He graduated became interested in body building, begin using steroids and became huge. Joining the police force was a huge accomplishment for him and he saw it as a way to get back at individuals that bullied him. Bullying in school does often occur in the teenage years. We saw visual evidence of this during the nineties, when students being bullied took measures into their own hands. Parents are now advocating stopping bullying in school, making the issue an enormous campaign because parents and educators alike feel it necessary to end this mishap before all our children end up victims of school gun violence.

Parenting

Rearing children is the greatest challenge mankind has to deal with, from centuries past and centuries to come, children evolve constantly through time and parents must deal with their children by being through the flexible. According to Santrock (2007, Ch 14) authoritative parenting best suits the way a child or a group of children should be raised.

Developing independence in children at an early age and encouraging a child to be his or her own individual, promotes self-awareness and responsibility in a child. This theory promotes such independence but at the same time there must be some limits and control put on the child. Our children are the pride of our hearts and we should treat them as such. Compared to the theory of authoritarian which place strict restriction of children and have no real person to person relationship with child and parent, the authoritative parenting style becomes the best method to go about using in bringing your child up in a healthy psychological way.

Chapter 12
Life and Death

Christians believe we are created and put on this earth for a purpose and we must have faith that God will lead us to this purpose. An issue in the field of life-span development that impacted my life is the one of death. In the last 5 years I have lost family members and people real close to me. The loss of relatives or friends can be a very hard time for anyone and I took it hard. However, it is life and this is the circle of life, we are born to die.

How one prepares for the transition of life and death is a question we are still searching answers for. Analytically looking at the situation I can recall my development from a child to young adulthood. As I think of those who have come and gone, I wonder to myself how were they prepared for that transition into the after-life.

The death of my grandmother struck me hard. Though she was elderly, it was bitter-sweet experience, in that she had finally gone home spiritually to rest. As a child we always looked up to our granny as a strong will woman. She was a giant to us and we felt she would forever be around. Unfortunately that is not how life works and to my knowledge that is a part of life-span and development. According to Santrock (2007) "Nonnormative life events are unusual occurrences that have a major impact on an individual's life." The life changing experience of losing granny brought me to a fast realization that we ought to love and take the best care of our loved ones while they are here. Letting our love one's smell the roses we want to give them while they are here is meaningful, especially when they have breath in their bodies to smell the scent. The impact such experiences have on you are forever. I will not ever be the same, the void of her not being here has filled my heart; but the love I have for her has helped heal that hurt somewhat.

In the arena of life-span and development according to Santrock (2007) "cognitive processes involve changes in the individual's thought, intelligence, and language." After losing my granny, I have found that my thinking towards life has changed because of how personally it has hit home. Dealing with such a loss has enabled me to be able to put myself in other's shoes and share their experiences in their time of lost and grief. In life we often hear that you cannot judge someone until you have walked in his or her shoes, and now I understand that when it comes to life and death. Loosing someone who has been in your life from birth does something to you. In a sense I am living for her and my ancestors from generations past. Cognitively as I now think of her passing, it has opened my mind to the fact that I will one day be gone and the life lessons I pass on is how I will be remembered.

Looking at life and death from an emotional perspective is painful. According to Santrock (2007) "Socio-emotional processes involve changes in the individual's relationships with other people, changes in emotions, and changes in personality." We knew our grandmother was getting older each day and year but the joy she brought to us and all that we learned from her in her time here, was well spent. Letting her go was and is still is a challenge. The advice and corrections she instilled in me, helped groom me into the man I am today.

The day I found out my grandmother had a stroke was weird in itself. I was at the park working out with my cousins and in the middle of my pull-up exercise I got stung in the eye by a bee. This was one of the worst most excruciating pains a person can ever endure. It was a shocker to me because I did not know where it came from. In our African, Liberian tribal tradition, such misfortune as this is a sign of a stroke or trouble in the family. I later found out that day from my mom that my grandma had a stroke and I broke down. Emotionally I was weak at that time because I knew her time was nearing the end. My value and relationship with my family members and friends has changed since then. Today a person can be here and gone tomorrow, neither a day nor a second is promised to us, that is why we must love for today.

A major issue surrounding life and death is that of euthanasia. Taking the life of another human is just inhumane. Mercy killing as they medically call it religiously goes against God's will for mankind. As a Christian I believe God uses suffering and misfortunes in people lives to fulfill his glory. The euthanizing of the elderly and seriously ill became a frequent practice at the turn of the century. The most recent incident of such a case is that of Terry Schiavo's. Shiavo became a quadriplegic for 15 years after she had a heart stoppage. Mr. Schiavo's, Terry's husband and his lawyers requested that Terry's feeding tube be removed allowing her to dehydrate (Byron Barlowe, 2009). Her parents and other opponents fought for the denial of the removal of Terry's tube in order to perceive the life she had. The court ruled in Mr. Schiavo favor and 15 days later after Terry's tube was removed she died. According to Sararson (1986) public interest for abortion and euthanasia have become an immoral act that have become accepted since World War II era. Sarason in his article talks about the case of young baby

Jane Doe and the decision of her parents to have her euthanatized. Jane Doe was born physically and mentally handicapped; her parents did not see if fit morally and financially to keep her alive. This controversial issue of life and death raised attention throughout the media world and brought out supporters for both stances. Supporters and opposition of Doe's decision were numerous and the story became frenzy.

In the field of Life-span and development the practice of euthanizing and abortion do not enhance the development of human life but instead hinders and destroys it. Trying to play the role of the great creator has brought a great misfortune to humanity. This practice of immorality has brought about a public debate and controversy that has reached the highest level of our courts. The death of my grandmother was hard to swallow, even though we knew her last days where nearing. I could not imagine my family choosing to euthanize granny because she was elderly and could not do much for herself anymore. Thus, the subject of life and death, abortion and euthanasia will continue to raise further debate in our courts, religious institutions, and psychologically.

Chapter 13
Examining the disorder of stuttering

The disorder of stuttering is inhabited by people from birth and occurs in their early stage of development. My understandings of stuttering begin early in my life, when I first noticed as a youth that my father had the disorder. As a child I did not know and could not comprehend why it was that dad words could not come out as quickly as he wanted them too. As a young child I took it to be funny and would poke fun of dad, until one day he got mad and give me a serious whipping.

My father is a highly intellectual man, with two masters and a doctoral degree in theology. As dad tells the story, he was born with fluent speech and as a child; his siblings had the habit of tickling one another, which became a constant habit that help lead to his stuttering disorder. Historically we have no one in our families that have stuttering problems and dad was the first to his knowledge of all his siblings to have developed this disorder.

According to mind disorder.com, "stuttering is defined as confusing and developmental speech and language disorder." Stuttering affects an individual fluency of speech and ability to convey their thought through everyday language. The simple language task that we take for granted, such as fluently being able to express one-self is a challenge for people who deal with stuttering disorder on a day to day basis. In the case of my father who stutters when he is mad or when he is trying to express a serious thought; he would usually begin with the words "um," "like," or "uh."

Based on psychological research and study, psychologist believes that stuttering is an inherited disease. In my father case, there are no historical accounts of anyone in our family having the disorder, other than him. The only theoretical conclusion that we as a family could come too, is that the tickling of him by his siblings led to the cause of his stuttering problem. My younger sister did in fact inherit the disorder from my father. Early in the first few years of her life, between the ages of which she begin to talk, she would stutter here and there. My grandmother believing in old African traditional ways of dealing with things told us when she would stutter, we should tap her on her back and she would get her words out. We sought that as an opportunity to haze our sister of her speech impediment. Whenever we heard my sister stuttering, we would give her a nice smack on her back. We often got a kick out of her situation, just being kids, but to our knowledge it actually worked. My younger sister grew out of the disorder that she had inherited.

Along with the disorder of stuttering, dis-fluency is much similar but is different in that it is produced by people who stutter, which deals with the sound and syllable repetitions of words. In such a case this is caused by the blockage of airflow. My fathers do not suffer from the disorder of dis-fluency. When you first meet him, you would not know he suffered from such a disorder but in conversation, when he is seriously trying to express himself, as I stated in previous paragraph, the disorder then become apparent.

Stuttering begins to show in most people in their early stage of development, between the age of two and five years old. During this stage the disease makes its self-evident, such in the case of my younger sister who begin showing signs of inherited stuttering. Stuttering does in fact occur later in life, due to cases such as a stroke or a degenerative neurological disease. According to mind disorder.com, "the primary symptoms of stuttering include excessive dis-fluency, both stuttering and normal types (core behaviors), as well as physical, emotional, and cognitive reactions to the problem." As I interviewed my father and asked him about how stuttering affected him emotional, he said he would get mad as a child when his peers made fun of him, which often resulted in a fight. This explains why my dad gave me a whipping that time as a child for poking fun at him. Stuttering does affect an individual self-esteem and confidence. As he grew older, his stuttering would improve however though.

Treating stuttering at an early age can offset the disorder and can stop the progression of the disease in the later years of the individual's life. According to mind disorder.com, "complete alleviation of recovery from stuttering is most likely possible when children and their families receive treatment close to the time of onset." Conducting intervention with the child as well with the family is the most effective way for the individual to recover from stuttering. For this mere reason the immediate treatment of the disorder is instrumental

Chapter 14

Developmental History Case Study

DEMOGRAPHIC INFORMATION

Child's Name
N/A_____

Date of Interview_9/26/09_____ Date of Birth__11/17/94_____ Age of child 14

Address N/A

Phone N/A

School Craigmont High School_ Grade 9

Teacher Mr. Miles   Male/Female__Male___

Referral Information:

Why are you seeking help for this child?

The child is smart and nothing psychological is wrong with him, he is just an old age baby.

Who referred you to our services?

This is a class case study

What kind of services are you seeking? (psychological or psychiatric testing, medical or physical exam, therapy)

Research study

PRIMARY CAREGIVER/PARENT INFORMATION

Father Name: Rev. Dr. Coker A.J George Jr.

Address (if different from mother) Memphis, TN

Phone N/A

Employment: Professor, Dean of Agriculture, the University of Liberia

Length of Employment: Recent employment this year

Occupation: Educator   Highest Grade Level: PHD in theology

Stepfather: N/A

Primary Language: English   Secondary Language: English

Mother Name: Patience M. George

Address (if different from father) Memphis, TN

Phone: N/A

Employment: Nurse, Regional Medical Center Memphis

Length of Employment: Ten Years

Occupation: <u>Nurse, RN</u> Highest Grade Level: <u>Master Degree, Business Administration</u>
Stepfather: <u>N/A</u>
Primary Language: <u>English</u> Secondary Language: <u>English</u>

Primary Caregiver

With what adults does this child live? <u>This child lives with both of his parents.</u>
How long in the current living situation? <u>He has lived with both parents his entire life.</u>
Name of Caregiver: Both parents as listed as above. <u>The Rev. Dr. George and Mrs. George.</u>
Relationship to Child: <u>Mother and Father</u>
Address: <u>Memphis, TN</u>
Age: <u>60 and 54</u>
Home Phone: <u>N/A</u> Work Phone: <u>N/A</u>
Occupation: <u>Professor and Nurse</u>
Employer: <u>University of Liberia and The Regional Medical Center</u>
How long with present employer<u>: Recently employed, mother 10 years with Medical Center</u>
Highest grade Completed<u>: Both parents, Masters and beyond</u>.
Primary Language: <u>English</u> Secondary Language: <u>English</u>

FAMILY HISTORY

Please list all brothers and sisters, and any other children living with the family

Age	Sex	Relationship to this child living at home?
35	**Male**	**Coker Tronkon George**
34	Female	Annie L. George Bailey
30	Female	Cokette Love George Gbaa
24	Male	Coker Jerome George III
22	Female	Rosette Deamah George
19	Female	Mardea H. George

CHILD CARE

If primary caregiver works outside the home, please provide the following information.
Who cares for this child when caregivers are gone? <u>None</u>
How many hours per day is this child in a child-care setting? <u>None</u>
How many different people care for this child? Please Explain. <u>None</u>

PREGNANCY

Planned pregnancy? ▫ * Yes x▫ No

Pregnancy under doctor's care: x▫ Yes ▫ No

Number of previous miscarriages:

<u>Check any of the following complications that occurred during the pregnancy</u>

▫ Difficulty in conception	▫ Toxemia	▫ Abnormal weight gain
▫ Measles	▫ Excessive vomiting	▫ German measles
▫ Excessive swelling	x▫ Emotional problems	▫ Vaginal bleeding
▫ Flu	▫ Anemia	▫ High blood pressure

Rh-incompatibility: None

Maternal injury: None

Describe_____

_____

Hospitalization during pregnancy: <u>None</u>

Reason: <u>None</u>

X-rays during pregnancy: <u>None</u>

Medications used during pregnancy: <u>Vitamins</u>

Alcohol used during pregnancy: <u>No</u>

Cigarettes during pregnancy: <u>No</u>

Other drugs used during pregnancy:

Type_____ Frequency_____ Prescription ▫ Yes ▫ No

Type_____ Frequency_____ Prescription ▫ Yes ▫ No

Type_____ Frequency_____ Prescription ▫ Yes ▫ No

Type_____ Frequency_____ Prescription ▫ Yes ▫ No

Type_____ Frequency_____ Prescription ▫ Yes ▫ No

Type_____ Frequency_____ Prescription ▫ Yes ▫ No

BIRTH

At this child's birth, what was the mother's age? <u>40</u> Fathers Age? <u>46</u>

Mother's age at birth of FIRST child? <u>31</u>

Was this child born in the hospital? x▫ Yes ▫ No

If No, where?_____

Length of pregnancy <u>9 months</u> Birth Weight: <u>9 pounds</u>

Length of Labor <u>15 hours</u> Apgar Score

Child's condition at birth Health 9 pounds.

Mother's condition at birth Healthy

Check any of the following complications that occurred during birth:

▢ Forceps used ▢ Breech Birth ▢ Labor Induced▢ Caesarean Delivery

Other Delivery Complications: _____

Incubator: ▢ Yes x▢ No How long? _____

Jaundiced: ▢ Yes x ▢ No Bilirubin Lights? ▢ Yes x ▢ No If Yes, How Long? _____

Breathing Problems right after birth: None

Supplemental Oxygen ▢ Yes x▢ No If yes, how long? _____

Was anesthesia used during delivery? ▢ Yes x▢ No If yes, what kind? _____

DEVELOPMENT

At what age did this child first do the following? Please indicate year/month of age.

Turn Over First few weeks of Life   Walk down Stairs At six months

Sit Alone At two and half three months   Show interest in or attraction to sound_____

Crawl Three months   Understand first words Four to Five months

Sand Alone Five and half months   Speak first words One years old

Walk Alone Six Months Speak in sentences Two to Three years old

Walk up Stairs Six months

Was this child breast-fed? x▢ Yes ▢ No When weaned?_____

Was this child bottle-fed? x▢ Yes ▢ No When weaned? _____

When was this child toilet trained? Before He was two years old Days_____ Nights

Did bed wetting occur after toilet training ▢ Yes x▢ No If yes, until what age? _____

Did bed-soling occur after toilet training? ▢ Yes x▢ No If yes, until what age? _____

Has this child experienced any of the following problems? If yes, please describe.

Walking difficulty: ▢ Yes x▢ No _____

Unclear Speech: ▢ Yes x▢ No _____

Sleep Problem: ▢ Yes x▢ No _____

Feeding Problem: ▢ Yes x▢ No _____

Underweight Problem: ▢ Yes x▢ No _____

Eating Problem: ▢ Yes x▢ No _____

Overweight Problem: ▢ Yes x▢ No _____

Colic: ▢ Yes x▢ No _____

Difficulty learning to Ride a Bike: ▢ Yes x▢ No _____

Difficulty Learning to Skip: ▢ Yes x▢ No _____

Difficulty Learning to Throw and Catch: ▢ Yes x▢ No _____

During this child's first four (4) years, were any special problems noted in the following areas? If yes, please describe.

Eating: ▢ Yes x▢ No _____

Motor skills: ▢ Yes x▢ No _____

Sleeping too much: ▢ Yes x▢ No _____

Temper tantrums: ▢ Yes x▢ No _____

Excessive crying: ▢ Yes x▢ No _____

Sleeping too little: ▢ Yes x▢ No _____

Failure to thrive: ▢ Yes x▢ No _____

Separating from parents: ▢ Yes x▢ No _____

Which hand does this child used for writing or drawing? <u>Right</u> Eating? <u>Right</u> Other?_____

Has this child been forced to change writing hand? ▢ Yes x▢ No

MEDICAL HISTORY

Childhood Illnesses/Injuries

Please check the illnesses this child has had and indicate age, year and month

Measles: x▢ Yes ▢ No_____   Rheumatic fever: ▢ Yes x▢ No_____

German measles: ▢ Yes x▢ No_____   Diphtheria: ▢ Yes x▢ No_____

Mumps: ▢ Yes x▢ No_____   Meningitis: ▢ Yes x▢ No_____

Chicken pox:x ▢ Yes ▢ No_____   Encephalitis: ▢ Yes x▢ No_____

Tuberculosis: ▢ Yes x▢ No_____   Anemia: ▢ Yes x▢ No_____

Whooping Cough: ▢ Yes x▢ No_____   Fever above 104^0: ▢ Yes x▢ No_____

Scarlet Fever: ▢ Yes x▢ No_____   Broken bone: ▢ Yes x▢ No_____

Head injury: ▢ Yes x▢ No_____   Sustained high fever: ▢ Yes x▢ No_____

Coma or any loss of consciousness: ▢ Yes x▢ No_____

Illness/Operations

Has this child ever been on any medication for six months or more? ▢ Yes x▢ No

Describe: <u>None</u>

<u>Please indicate whether this child currently has any of the following problems.</u>

Respiratory
▢ Frequent colds
▢ Chronic cough
▢ Asthma
▢ Hay fever
x▢ Sinus condition

Cardiovascular
▢ Shortness of breath
▢ Dizziness with physical exertion
▢ Activity limited due to heart
▢ Condition
▢ Heart murmur

Gastrointestinal
▢ Excessive vomiting
▢ Frequent diarrhea
▢ Constipation
▢ Stomach pain

Genitourinary
▢ Urination in pants/bed
▢ Pain while urinating
▢ Excessive urination
▢ Strong odor to urine

Musculosketetal
▢ Muscle pain
▢ Clumsy walk
▢ Poor posture
▢ Other muscle problems

Neurological
▢ Seizures/convulsions
▢ Speech defects
▢ Bites nails
▢ Sucks thumb
▢ Tics/twitches
▢ Bangs head
▢ Rocks back and forth

Allergies
▢ Allergy to medicine

▢ Allergy to Food
▢ Bowel movements in other allergies

Skin
x▢ Frequent rashes
  <u>Breaks out easily</u>
▢ Bruises easily
▢ Sores

▫ Pants/bed   ▫ Severe acne

                                                     ▫ Itchy skin (Eczema)

Speech	*Hearing*	*Vision*
▫ Stuttering	▫ Ear infections	▫ Vision problems
▫ Unclear speech	▫ Hearing problems	▫ Glasses/contacts
▫ Other speech problems	▫ Ear tubes	

Date of most recent speech exam: _____

Date of most recent hearing exam: _____

Date of most recent vision exam: _____

MEDICAL CARE

Child's Physician: Dr. Smith

How often does child see doctor? <u>Twice a year</u>

Is this child currently on medication? ▫ Yesx ▫ No_____

Has this child ever been physically or sexually abused or neglected? <u>No</u>

Has this child ever had psychological counseling or therapy? <u>No</u>

Has this child ever had a neurological exam? <u>No</u>

Has this child ever had a psychological or psychiatric exam? <u>No</u>

If yes, persons name, date of exam, reason for exam, telephone number of person: <u>None</u>

Chapter 15

Genogram

The role of responsibility of parents in the lives of their child or children is instrumental for the psychological healthy development of the child. The bond and relationship of a mother and child is a bond that is essential to the psychological health of a child. That motherly love and learning the importance of affection and care develops a sense of importance of the relationship.

Having a mother of such a great heart and character and love for a family makes you believe that Angels do exist in the world.   Early in life the role mom, Patience M. George played was immediately established, from the way she conducted tasks in our lives. The way she conducted our lives and her life as well was like an orchestra. She always had things under control, no matter what the situation or the circumstances were. Always keeping a cool decorum of how she went about her business, mom did what she had to do for her family and friends. For the most of my life mom took care of individuals that were not her own children. Friends and sometimes family members would send their child or children to live with my parents, in order for them to come up in a positive home and environment. Throughout my life all I have seen is my mother taking care of people and being a blessing to her fellow human being. While living in Liberia, before we moved to the United States and mother became a nurse, she acted as a nurse in Liberia. When individuals in the community would get sick, mother would take care of them or see to it that they got the proper care. My grandmother was a nurse and mother would do what she could, until grandma was able to get to them. Those events in my early life were foretelling events to what mother would later become in life. In coming to America, mother continued her natural life mission efforts of taking care of people and mankind in general. Her work would continue in her convergence of our first home into a daycare, while she looked for work and while dad attended the Memphis Theological Seminary. Mother then returned to school, where she begin working on her next degree of becoming a registered nurse. She would earn her degree and begin her lifelong goal of care taking of people who are ill. If mother is an Angel on earth, so is my father Rev. Dr. Coker A.J. George Jr. From early on in life, I believe my parents were a match made in heaven to carry out God's mission on earth. The similarities their lives shared were enormous. The traits I have are both equal of that of both my parents. Dad is the most giving and willing person I know, in that he will take the shirt off his back for anyone. From the time I have known my father, all he has ever done is been a blessing to people. For a great number of years, early in my young life, my father was the bread winning for his side of the family as well as mother side. During the civil war that took place in Liberia in the late eighties and throughout the nineties, was when I first begin to notice the saint like characteristics of my father, and both parents alike. When the rebels took over and where capturing people and executing them for secular and discriminatory reasons; dad would put his life and his family life as well on the line and plea for the lives of those individuals appointed to die by the rebels. I can recall on numerous accounts in which God used his divine intervention through dad. Our transition of life to America became the extension for God mission for Dad. Coming to the United States to study theology and to show his self a proof to preach the word of God became his next calling. Our early life in America was quite a transition that dad help make smooth because he had previously lived in these United States of America. The first couple of months as well as years were quite a challenge. Dad would become a youth director at the local United Methodist Church and then attend school full-time. The love and relationship the youth of the program had for dad as well as mom was a relationship better then relationships most the children had for their own parents. Being comforting and making people feel at home is how dad and mom treated people, which make it rare for a person not to become comfortable in such an environment. The love and bonding relationship I have with my parents is a beautiful. Early in life that relationship was strong and just as most parents, who are raising their children in the way he or she should grow, will encounter those hard adolescent years, in which you and your parents seem as enemies. When I became a man and begin to do those things that made my parents proud, such as matriculating through college and advancing to the next level of education and taking on a lot of responsibilities, the relationship between us grew closer and took on a whole other level of respect between both parties. We do not always get along with our parents and I sometimes don't get along with mom and dad, when they feel as if I am not reaching my full potential. In understanding life from the various perspectives that I have been able to experience it from, I now have the will and persistence of mother, not to give up on people and to believe in an individual's willingness to change or want a better life for him or herself. Both of my parents possess these characteristics, it is just that mother would stick by your side, to the ultimate end, especially when you seem down and out. I am much like my father in that we both possess the ability and the quest for achievement. My genes and yearning ability and will to achieve in every field of human endeavor comes directly from my father. The manner in which I push myself is along the same lines and the same standard in which I hold myself. Mom ability to not be seriously bothered by stress and life burdens and circumstances is like no other. It seems as if she has a natural stress blocker in her mind, I still wonder how she does it. This ability I believe I have gradually developed. Being able to bring the best out of people is my father's gift. Dad has the ability to have people believe in a cause and themselves as well. Communication is the key to life and dad can relay a message to a group of people or an individual and it will be highly comprehended. Both of my parents are my role models and early in my life I did not truly understand why the really were. I can recall my dad and me having an argument over why I should not view athletes or stars as my role models and they my parents ought to be my major role models. The upstanding and Godly manor in which Dr. and Mrs. George live their lives is the way in which I plan to live my life. Learning how a man or a woman should treat one another is one of the greatest assets a child can develop from a mother-father relationship. Mom and dad were not overly affectionate but were however loving and extremely caring for one another. The level of respect they have for one another, each individual letting his or her partner play their roles in the relationship has been the key to the success of their marriage. A man or a woman learns by experiences, based on the cognitive theory according to Santrock (2007). Having such a positive example of how a man or a woman shall treat their spouse, my siblings and I have been groomed for life, how to conduct our personal and romantic relationships. I know from watchful experience that a man is supposed to adore his wife and she is supposed to respect and cherish her husband. My father treated

my mother like the queen she deserved to be treated as. I have thus been able to gain this

same trait and been able to portray that in the relationships I have had.

Reference

Stuttering.Retrieved from: http://www.minddisorders.com/Py-Z/Stuttering.html#ixzzoUDyQFvUT

Santrock, W, J. (2007). A topical approach to life-span development. [University of Phoenix Custom 3rd Edition e-text Ch. 1]. The McGraw-Hill Companies. Retrieved September 9,-October 2009, from University of Phoenix, rEsource, PSYCH500-Lifespan Development Course Web site.